DIEN CAI DAU

Also by Yusef Komunyakaa

DIEN CAI DAU

Yusef Komunyakaa

WESLEYAN UNIVERSITY PRESS
Middletown, Connecticut

Published by Wesleyan University Press
Middletown, CT 06459
www.wesleyan.edu/wespress

Printed in the United States of America
15 14 13 12 11 10

WESLEYAN POETRY
First printing, 1988

Grateful acknowledgment is made to the following publications in which these poems first appeared: *Alcatraz, The American Voice, AWP Newsletter, Caliban, Callaloo, Cincinnati Poetry Review, Colorado Review, Indiana Review, The Louisiana Weekly, MSS, New England Review and Bread Loaf Quarterly, The North American Review, Ploughshares, Shankpainter, Writers Forum*. Some of these poems also appeared in a limited edition chapbook, *Toys in a Field* (Black River Press, 1986). Acknowledgment is also made to the following anthologies: *The Morrow Anthology of Younger American Poets*: "Somewhere Near Phu Bai," "Starlight Scope Myopia"; *Carrying the Darkness*: "After the Fall," "The Dead at Quang Tri," "A Break from the Bush," "Boat People," "Somewhere Near Phu Bai"; *The Made Thing*: "We Never Know," "Saigon Bar Girls, 1975," "Facing It."

I wish to thank the Louisiana Arts Commission for a fellowship that enabled me to complete this book.

LIBRARY OF CONGRESS CATALOGING-IN-PUBLICATION DATA
Komunyakaa, Yusef.
Dien Cai Dau.
1. Vietnamese Conflict, 1961–1975—Poetry.   I. Title.
PS3561.O455D5   1988   811'.54   88-5761
ISBN 0-8195-2163-9
ISBN 0-8195-1164-1 (pbk.)

for my brother Glenn
who saw The Nam before I did

Contents

DIEN CAI DAU

Camouflaging the Chimera

We tied branches to our helmets.
We painted our faces & rifles
with mud from a riverbank,

blades of grass hung from the pockets
of our tiger suits. We wove
ourselves into the terrain,
content to be a hummingbird's target.

We hugged bamboo & leaned
against a breeze off the river,
slow-dragging with ghosts

from Saigon to Bangkok,
with women left in doorways
reaching in from America.
We aimed at dark-hearted songbirds.

In our way station of shadows
rock apes tried to blow our cover,
throwing stones at the sunset. Chameleons

crawled our spines, changing from day
to night: green to gold,
gold to black. But we waited
till the moon touched metal,

till something almost broke
inside us. VC struggled
with the hillside, like black silk

wrestling iron through grass.
We weren't there. The river ran
through our bones. Small animals took refuge
against our bodies; we held our breath,

ready to spring the L-shaped
ambush, as a world revolved
under each man's eyelid.

Tunnels

Crawling down headfirst into the hole,
he kicks the air & disappears.
I feel like I'm down there
with him, moving ahead, pushed
by a river of darkness, feeling
blessed for each inch of the unknown.
Our tunnel rat is the smallest man
in the platoon, in an echo chamber
that makes his ears bleed
when he pulls the trigger.
He moves as if trying to outdo
blind fish easing toward imagined blue,
pulled by something greater than life's
ambitions. He can't think about
spiders & scorpions mending the air,
or care about bats upside down
like gods in the mole's blackness.
The damp smell goes deeper
than the stench of honey buckets.
A web of booby traps waits, ready
to spring into broken stars.
Forced onward by some need,
some urge, he knows the pulse
of mysteries & diversions
like thoughts trapped in the ground.
He questions each root.
Every cornered shadow has a life
to bargain with. Like an angel
pushed up against what hurts,
his globe-shaped helmet
follows the gold ring his flashlight
casts into the void. Through silver
lice, shit, maggots, & vapor of pestilence,

he goes, the good soldier,
on hands & knees, tunneling past
death sacked into a blind corner,
loving the weight of the shotgun
that will someday dig his grave.

Somewhere Near Phu Bai

The moon cuts through
night trees like a circular saw
white hot. In the guard shack
I lean on the sandbags,
taking aim at whatever.
Hundreds of blue-steel stars
cut a path, fanning out
silver for a second. If anyone's
there, don't blame me.

I count the shapes ten meters
out front, over & over, making sure
they're always there.
I don't dare blink an eye.
The white-painted backs
of the Claymore mines
like quarter-moons.
They say Victor Charlie will
paint the other sides & turn
the blast toward you.

If I hear a noise
will I push the button
& blow myself away?
The moon grazes treetops.
I count the Claymores again.
Thinking about buckshot
kneaded in the plastic C-4
of the brain, counting
sheep before I know it.

Starlight Scope Myopia

Gray-blue shadows lift
shadows onto an oxcart.

Making night work for us,
the starlight scope brings
men into killing range.

The river under Vi Bridge
takes the heart away

like the Water God
riding his dragon.
Smoke-colored

Viet Cong
move under our eyelids,

lords over loneliness
winding like coral vine through
sandalwood & lotus,

inside our lowered heads
years after this scene

ends. The brain closes
down. What looks like
one step into the trees,

they're lifting crates of ammo
& sacks of rice, swaying

under their shared weight.
Caught in the infrared,
what are they saying?

Are they talking about women
or calling the Americans

beaucoup dien cai dau?
One of them is laughing.
You want to place a finger

to his lips & say "shhhh."
You try reading ghost talk

on their lips. They say
"up-up we go," lifting as one.
This one, old, bowlegged,

you feel you could reach out
& take him into your arms. You

peer down the sights of your M-16,
seeing the full moon
loaded on an oxcart.

Red Pagoda

Our eyes on the hill,
we have to get there
somehow. Three snipers
sing out like hornets.
The red pawn's our last move—
green & yellow squares
backdropped with mangrove
swamps, something to hold to.
Hand over hand, we follow
invisible rope to nowhere,
duck-walking through grass
& nosing across the line
of no return. Remnants
of two thatch huts tremble
to heavy, running feet.
We make it to the hill,
fall down & slide rounds
into the mortar tube,
& smithereens of leaf debris
cover the snipers. Unscathed,
with arms hooked through each other's
like men on some wild
midnight-bound carousal,
in our joy, we kick
& smash the pagoda
till it's dried blood
covering the ground.

A Greenness Taller Than Gods

When we stop,
a green snake starts again
through deep branches.
Spiders mend webs we marched into.
Monkeys jabber in flame trees,
dancing on the limbs to make
fire-colored petals fall. Torch birds
burn through the dark-green day.
The lieutenant puts on sunglasses
& points to an X circled
on his map. When will we learn
to move like trees move?
The point man raises his hand *Wait*!
We've just crossed paths with VC,
branches left quivering.
The lieutenant's right hand says what to do.
We walk into a clearing that blinds.
We move like a platoon of silhouettes
balancing sledge hammers on our heads,
unaware our shadows have untied
from us, wandered off
& gotten lost.

The Dead at Quang Tri

This is harder than counting stones
along paths going nowhere, the way
a tiger circles & backtracks by
smelling his blood on the ground.
The one kneeling beside the pagoda,
remember him? Captain, we won't
talk about that. The Buddhist boy
at the gate with the shaven head
we rubbed for luck
glides by like a white moon.
He won't stay dead, dammit!
Blades aim for the family jewels;
the grass we walk on
won't stay down.

Hanoi Hannah

Ray Charles! His voice
calls from waist-high grass,
& we duck behind gray sandbags.
"Hello, Soul Brothers. Yeah,
Georgia's also on my mind."
Flares bloom over the trees.
"Here's Hannah again.
Let's see if we can't
light her goddamn fuse
this time." Artillery
shells carve a white arc
against dusk. Her voice rises
from a hedgerow on our left.
"It's Saturday night in the States.
Guess what your woman's doing tonight.
I think I'll let Tina Turner
tell you, you homesick GIs."
Howitzers buck like a herd
of horses behind concertina.
"You know you're dead men,
don't you? You're dead
as King today in Memphis.
Boys, you're surrounded by
General Tran Do's division."
Her knife-edge song cuts
deep as a sniper's bullet.
"Soul Brothers, what you dying for?"
We lay down a white-klieg
trail of tracers. Phantom jets
fan out over the trees.
Artillery fire zeros in.
Her voice grows flesh
& we can see her falling
into words, a bleeding flower

no one knows the true name for.
"You're lousy shots, GIs."
Her laughter floats up
as though the airways are
buried under our feet.

Roll Call

Through rifle sights
we must've looked like crows
perched on a fire-eaten branch,
lined up for reveille, ready
to roll-call each M-16
propped upright
between a pair of jungle boots,
a helmet on its barrel
as if it were a man.
The perfect row aligned
with the chaplain's cross
while a metallic-gray squadron
of sea gulls circled. Only
a few lovers have blurred
the edges of this picture.
Sometimes I can hear them
marching through the house,
closing the distance. All
the lonely beds take me back
to where we saluted those
five pairs of boots
as the sun rose against our faces.

Fragging

Five men pull straws
under a tree on a hillside.
Damp smoke & mist halo them
as they single out each other,
pretending they're not there.
"We won't be wasting a real man.
That lieutenant's too gung ho.
Think, man, 'bout how Turk
got blown away; next time
it's you or me. Hell,
the truth is the truth."
Something small as a clinch pin
can hold men together,
humming their one-word
song. Yes, just a flick
of a wrist & the whole night
comes apart. "Didn't we warn him?
That bastard." "Remember, Joe,
remember how he pushed Perez?"
The five men breathe like a wave
of cicadas, their bowed heads
filled with splintered starlight.
They uncoil fast as a fist.
Looking at the ground, four
walk north, then disappear. One
comes this way, moving through
a bad dream. Slipping a finger
into the metal ring, he's married
to his devil—the spoon-shaped
handle flies off. Everything
breaks for green cover,
like a hundred red birds
released from a wooden box.

"You and I Are Disappearing"
—Björn Håkansson

The cry I bring down from the hills
belongs to a girl still burning
inside my head. At daybreak
    she burns like a piece of paper.
She burns like foxfire
in a thigh-shaped valley.
A skirt of flames
dances around her
at dusk.
       We stand with our hands
hanging at our sides,
while she burns
    like a sack of dry ice.
She burns like oil on water.
She burns like a cattail torch
dipped in gasoline.
She glows like the fat tip
of a banker's cigar,
    silent as quicksilver.
A tiger under a rainbow
   at nightfall.
She burns like a shot glass of vodka.
She burns like a field of poppies
at the edge of a rain forest.
She rises like dragonsmoke
   to my nostrils.
She burns like a burning bush
driven by a godawful wind.

2527th Birthday of the Buddha

When the motorcade rolled to a halt, Quang Duc
climbed out & sat down in the street.
He crossed his legs,
& the other monks & nuns grew around him like petals.
He challenged the morning sun,
debating with the air
he leafed through—visions brought down to earth.
Could his eyes burn the devil out of men?
A breath of peppermint oil
soothed someone's cry. Beyond terror made flesh—
he burned like a bundle of black joss sticks.
A high wind that started in California
fanned flames, turned each blue page,
leaving only his heart intact.
Waves of saffron robes bowed to the gasoline can.

Re-creating the Scene

The metal door groans
& folds shut like an ancient turtle
that won't let go
of a finger till it thunders.
The Confederate flag
flaps from a radio antenna,
& the woman's clothes
come apart in their hands.
Their mouths find hers
in the titanic darkness
of the steel grotto,
as she counts the names of dead
ancestors, shielding a baby
in her arms. The three men
ride her breath, grunting
over lovers back in Mississippi.
She floats on their rage
like a torn water flower,
defining night inside a machine
where men are gods.
The season quietly sweats.
They hold her down
with their eyes,
taking turns, piling stones
on her father's grave.
The APC rolls with curves of the land,
up hills & down into gullies,
crushing trees & grass,
droning like a constellation
of locusts eating through bamboo,
creating the motion for their bodies.

She rises from the dust
& pulls the torn garment
around her, staring after the APC
till it's small enough
to fit like a toy tank in her hands.
She turns in a circle,
pounding the samarium dust
with her feet where the steel
tracks have plowed. The sun
fizzes like a pill in a glass
of water, & for a moment
the world's future tense:
She approaches the MPs
at the gate; a captain from G-5
accosts her with candy kisses;
I inform *The Overseas Weekly*;
flashbulbs refract her face
in a room of polished brass
& spit-shined boots;
on the trial's second day
she turns into mist—
someone says money
changed hands,
& someone else swears
she's buried at LZ Gator.
But for now, the baby
makes a fist & grabs at the air,
searching for a breast.

Night Muse & Mortar Round

She shows up in every war.
Basically the same, maybe
her flowing white gown's a little less
erotic & she's more desperate.
She's always near a bridge.
This time the Perfume River.
You trace the curve in the road
& there she is

trying to flag down your jeep,
but you're a quarter-mile away
when you slam on the brakes.
Sgt. Jackson says, "What the hell
you think you're doing, Jim?"
& Lt. Adonis riding shotgun
yells, "Court-martial."

When you finally drive back
she's gone, just a feeling
left in the night air.
Then you hear the blast
rock the trees & stars
where you would've been that moment.

One More Loss to Count

"Me, I'm Chinese,"
Be Hai says.
She's the sergeant major's woman,
switching from French to English.
We talk with our eyes,
sipping Cokes in my hooch.
Days pass before she shows up again
with a shy look, not herself,
that bowed dance with her head
the Vietnamese do.
Sometimes I look up to find
her standing in the doorway,
not knowing how long
she's been there, watching me
with my earphones plugged in
to James Brown or Aretha,
her man somewhere sleeping off
another all-night drunk.
Once I asked her about family.
"Not important, GI," she said.

We all have our ghosts.
Mine are Anna's letters from L.A.
This morning Be Hai shows up
with a photograph of the sergeant major
& his blond children
back in Alabama.
For months we've dodged
each other in this room,
dancers with bamboo torches.
She clutches the snapshot like a pass
to enter an iron-spiked gate.
There's nothing else to say.
The room's caught up in our movement,

& the novel Anna sent me days ago
slides from the crowded shelf.
Like the cassette rewinding
we roll back the words in our throats.
She closes her eyes, the photograph
falls from her hand
like the ace of spades
shadowing a pale leaf.

Sappers

Opium, horse, nothing
sends anybody through concertina
this way. What is it in the brain
that so totally propels a man?
Caught with women in our heads
three hours before daybreak,
we fire full automatic
but they keep coming,
slinging satchel charges
at our bunkers. They fall
& rise again like torchbearers,
with their naked bodies
greased so moonlight dances
off their skin. They run
with explosives strapped
around their waists,
& try to fling themselves
into our arms.

Nude Pictures

I slapped him a third time.
The song caught in his throat
for a second, & the morning
came back together like after
a stone has been dropped
through a man's reflection
hiding in a river. I slapped him
again, but he wouldn't stop

laughing. As we searched
for the squad, he drew us
to him like a marsh loon
tied to its half-gone song
echoing over rice fields
& through wet elephant grass
smelling of gunpowder & fear.
I slapped him once more.

Booby-trapped pages floated
through dust. His laughter
broke off into a silence
early insects touched
with a tinge of lost music.
He grabbed my hand & wouldn't
let go. Lifted by a breeze,
a face danced in the treetops.

We Never Know

He danced with tall grass
for a moment, like he was swaying
with a woman. Our gun barrels
glowed white-hot.
When I got to him,
a blue halo
of flies had already claimed him.
I pulled the crumbled photograph
from his fingers.
There's no other way
to say this: I fell in love.
The morning cleared again,
except for a distant mortar
& somewhere choppers taking off.
I slid the wallet into his pocket
& turned him over, so he wouldn't be
kissing the ground.

A Break from the Bush

The South China Sea
drives in another herd.
The volleyball's a punching bag:
Clem's already lost a tooth
& Johnny's left eye is swollen shut.
Frozen airlifted steaks burn
on a wire grill, & miles away
machine guns can be heard.
Pretending we're somewhere else,
we play harder.
Lee Otis, the point man,
high on Buddha grass,
buries himself up to his neck
in sand. "Can you see me now?
In this spot they gonna build
a Hilton. Invest in Paradise.
Bang, bozos! You're dead."
Frenchie's cassette player
unravels Hendrix's "Purple Haze."
Snake, 17, from Daytona,
sits at the water's edge,
the ash on his cigarette
pointing to the ground
like a crooked finger. CJ,
who in three days will trip
a fragmentation mine,
runs after the ball
into the whitecaps,
laughing.

Seeing in the Dark

The scratchy sound of skin
flicks works deeper & deeper,
as mortar fire colors the night
flesh tone. The corporal at the door
grins; his teeth shiny as raw pearl,
he stands with a fist of money,
happy to see infantrymen
from the boonies—men who know
more about dodging trip wires &
seeing in the dark than they do
about women. They're in Shangri-la
gaping at washed-out images
thrown against a bedsheet.

We're men ready to be fused
with ghost pictures, trying
to keep the faces we love
from getting shuffled
with those on the wall.
Is that Hawk's tenor
coloring-in the next frame?
Three women on a round bed
coax in a German shepherd—
everything turns white as alabaster.
The picture flickers; the projector
goes dead, & we cuss the dark
& the cicadas' heavy breath.

Tu Do Street

Music divides the evening.
I close my eyes & can see
men drawing lines in the dust.
America pushes through the membrane
of mist & smoke, & I'm a small boy
again in Bogalusa. *White Only*
signs & Hank Snow. But tonight
I walk into a place where bar girls
fade like tropical birds. When
I order a beer, the mama-san
behind the counter acts as if she
can't understand, while her eyes
skirt each white face, as Hank Williams
calls from the psychedelic jukebox.
We have played Judas where
only machine-gun fire brings us
together. Down the street
black GIs hold to their turf also.
An off-limits sign pulls me
deeper into alleys, as I look
for a softness behind these voices
wounded by their beauty & war.
Back in the bush at Dak To
& Khe Sanh, we fought
the brothers of these women
we now run to hold in our arms.
There's more than a nation
inside us, as black & white
soldiers touch the same lovers
minutes apart, tasting
each other's breath,
without knowing these rooms
run into each other like tunnels
leading to the underworld.

Communiqué

Bob Hope's on stage, but we want the Gold Diggers,
want a flash of legs

through the hemorrhage of vermilion, giving us
something to kill for.

We want our hearts wrung out like rags & ground down
to Georgia dust

while Cobras drag the perimeter, gliding along the sea,
swinging searchlights

through the trees. The assault & battery of hot pink
glitter erupts

as the rock 'n' roll band tears down the night—caught
in a safety net

of brightness, The Gold Diggers convulse. White legs
shimmer like strobes.

The lead guitarist's right foot's welded to his wah-wah.
"I thought you said

Aretha was gonna be here." "Man, I don't wanna see
no Miss America."

"There's Lola." The sky is blurred by magnesium flares
over the fishing boats.

"Shit, man, she looks awful white to me." We duck
when we hear the quick

metallic hiss of the mountain of amplifiers struck by
a flash of rain.

After the show's packed up & gone, after the choppers
have flown out backwards,

after the music & colors have died slowly in our heads,
& the downpour's picked up,

we sit holding our helmets like rain-polished skulls.

The Edge

When guns fall silent for an hour
or two, you can hear the cries

of women making love to soldiers.
They have an unmerciful memory

& know how to wear bright dresses
to draw a crowd, conversing

with a platoon of shadows
numbed by morphine. Their real feelings

make them break like April
into red blossoms.

Cursing themselves in ragged dreams
fire has singed the edges of,

they know a slow dying the fields have come to terms with.
Shimmering fans work against the heat

& smell of gunpowder, making money
float from hand to hand. The next moment

a rocket pushes a white fist
through night sky, & they scatter like birds

& fall into the shape their lives
have become.

"You want a girl, GI?"
"You buy me Saigon tea?"

Soldiers bring the scent of burning flesh
with them—on their clothes & in their hair,

drawn to faces in half-lit rooms.
As good-bye kisses are thrown

to the charred air, silhouettes of jets
ease over nude bodies on straw mats.

Donut Dollies

The three stood outside Toc
smiling, waiting with donuts & coffee
for the dusty-green platoon
back from a fire fight,
as the midday sun
fell through their sky-
blue dresses with Red Cross
insignia over their breasts,
like half-hearted cheerleaders.
But the GIs filed past them
with night-long tracer glare
still in their eyes
& the names of dead men
caught in their throats.
Across the hills a recoilless rifle
& mortar spoke to each other.
They followed a thousand-yard stare
until they walked out of boots & fatigues
& fled into the metal stalls
to shower off the night.
For days the donut dollies
were unable to stop shaking
their heads, like a ripple
trembling through horses.
Even back at the Officers' Club
they couldn't pull their eyes away
from the line of infantrymen
dragging their tired feet,
molded into a slow melody
inside bowed heads. They
were unable to feel the hands
slip under their uniforms & touch
money belts next to their pale skin.

Prisoners

Usually at the helipad
I see them stumble-dance
across the hot asphalt
with crokersacks over their heads,
moving toward the interrogation huts,
thin-framed as box kites
of sticks & black silk
anticipating a hard wind
that'll tug & snatch them
out into space. I think
some must be laughing
under their dust-colored hoods,
knowing rockets are aimed
at Chu Lai—that the water's
evaporating & soon the nail
will make contact with metal.
How can anyone anywhere love
these half-broken figures
bent under the sky's brightness?
The weight they carry
is the soil we tread night & day.
Who can cry for them?
I've heard the old ones
are the hardest to break.
An arm twist, a combat boot
against the skull, a .45
jabbed into the mouth, nothing
works. When they start talking
with ancestors faint as camphor
smoke in pagodas, you know
you'll have to kill them
to get an answer.
Sunlight throws
scythes against the afternoon.

Everything's a heat mirage; a river
tugs at their slow feet.
I stand alone & amazed,
with a pill-happy door gunner
signaling for me to board the Cobra.
I remember how one day
I almost bowed to such figures
walking toward me, under
a corporal's ironclad stare.
I can't say why.
From a half-mile away
trees huddle together,
& the prisoners look like
marionettes hooked to strings of light.

Jungle Surrender
after Don Cooper's painting

Ghosts share us with the past & future
but we struggle to hold on to each breath.

Moving toward what waits behind the trees,
the prisoner goes deeper into himself, away

from how a man's heart divides him, deeper
into the jungle's indigo mystery & beauty,

with both hands raised into the air, only
surrendering halfway: the small man inside

waits like a photo in a shirt pocket, refusing
to raise his hands, silent & uncompromising

as the black scout dog beside him. Love & hate
flesh out the real man, how he wrestles

himself through a hallucination of blues
& deep purples that set the day on fire.

He sleepwalks a labyrinth of violet,
measuring footsteps from one tree to the next,

knowing we're all somehow connected.
What would I have said?

The real interrogator is a voice within.
I would have told them about my daughter

in Phoenix, how young she was,
about my first woman, anything

but how I helped ambush two Viet Cong
while plugged into the Grateful Dead.

For some, a soft windy voice makes them
snap. Blues & purples. Some place between

central Georgia & Tay Ninh Province—
the vision a knot of blood unravels

& parts of us we dared put into the picture
come together; the prisoner goes away

almost whole. But he will always touch
fraying edges of things, to feel hope break

like the worm that rejoins itself
under the soil . . . head to tail.

Eyeball Television

He sits crouched in a hole
covered with slats of bamboo,
recalling hundreds of faces
from *I Love Lucy, Dragnet,*
I Spy, & *The Ed Sullivan Show.*
A pinhole of light tells
when day comes. Sound
reaches him like honeybees
trapped in a boy's Coke bottle.
When he can't stop laughing
at *Roadrunner* on Channel 6
the sharp pain goes away.
Holding the world in focus
in his solitary cell, he sees
Spike Jones' one-man band
explode. Two minutes later
Marilyn Monroe is nude
on a round white sofa
that dissolves into a cloud.
Shaking his head to get her pose
right again, he finds himself
pushing vertical & horizontal hold
buttons, but only Liberace's
piano eases into the disconnected
landscape. He hears deliberate,
heavy footsteps of the guards
coming for him. The picture
fades into the sound of urine
dripping on his forehead,
as he tries to read the lips of Walter Cronkite.

The One-legged Stool

Semidarkness. A black POW is seated on a one-legged stool. He looks all round, slowly stands, then lets the stool hit the dirt floor. He's in a state of delirium, partly hallucinating. Periodically a shadow of a face appears at the peephole in the door.

You didn't see that. My stool never touched the floor, guard. I'm still sitting on my stool. It's all in your head. Would you just drag me out into the compound, then put a bullet through my brains for nothing? Do you call that honor? I never left my stool! It never touched the fucking floor! Look, I've been sitting here hypnotized by dawn crawling under the door like a bamboo viper. (*Pause.*) Sometimes there's a distant bird singing just for me. That's right. Just for me. I sit here on this one-legged stool, watching your eyes pressed against the face-window. Don't you know I'll never cooperate? No, don't care what you whisper into the darkness of this cage like it came out of my own head, I won't believe a word. Lies, lies, lies. You're lying. Those white prisoners didn't say what you say they said. They ain't laughing. Ain't cooperating. They ain't putting me down, calling me names like you say. Lies. Lies. It ain't the way you say it is. I'm American. (*Pause.*) Doctor King, he ain't dead like you say. Lies. How many times are you trying to kill me? Twice, three times, four, how many? You can't break me. Drops of water beating on my head for weeks, that didn't work. Bamboo under my fingernails, that didn't work either. The month I laid cramped in that body-cave of yours, with a pain running through me like a live wire, that didn't make me talk into your microphone. (*Pause.*) What you say? You gook, dink, slant-eyed sloe! That's right. I can get nasty too, just as cruel, you bastard. Standing there with your face in the window like a yellow moon that never goes down. I can give the devil hell. I can be Don Quixote fighting fields of windmills. You should've seen me at Khe Sanh! You think you're bad? Shit. Our machine gunner, Johnson, a kid we called Chi, he got hit. I took his M-60, walked that burning hill for a solid straight hour with the Pig. Charlies didn't know what to do. I was dancing, swaying with that machine gun. (*Pause.*) You didn't see that. The hand's quicker than the eye. You didn't see that. I'm still sitting on my stool. I sleep, I live here on my damn stool. (*Pause.*) You've pitted me against them. Against those white troops over there behind those trees. I only half hear their voices through these bamboo walls. For my good, huh? You really think I believe that shit? I know how to protect myself, you can bet your life on that. I also know your games, VC. Anything to break a man, right? Anything to grind his mind to dust. But I know how to walk out of a nightmare backwards. I can survive. When you kicked me awake, then back into a stupor, did I break? Maybe I slipped back a few feet deeper into the darkness, but I didn't break. Maybe I pulled back into myself. Pulled back till there's nowhere to go. Sometimes it's like holding back a flood, but I'm still standing here. Crouched in this place, just listening to my stupid heart. With you always two steps away, always so goddamn close, listening to my thoughts. Sometimes I can hear empty locust shells crack under my feet when I was a boy, but I'm not broken yet. (*Pause.*) I wasn't scratching for earthworms. I was sitting here, not batting an eyelid. I wasn't sniffing the ground like a dog on all fours. That wasn't me. Your eyes must be tricking you or something. Watch this. Do you see that dung beetle? Look! You see, the hands are quicker than the eyes. You didn't see me eat that bug, did you? No, don't think about how the dampness in here hurts. Just concentrate. (*Roars with laughter.*) You know what I was thinking? I was thinking a hundred ways I could bury you. Charlie, you can kill me, you can turn me into an animal, you can make me wish I was never born, but you can't break me. I won't cooperate. (*Pause.*) You didn't see that. I'm still sitting here on my stool. Name, rank—Sergeant First Class Thomas J. Washington. Serial number—321-45-

9876. Mission—try to keep alive. (*Pause.*) Yeah, VC. I've been through Georgia. Yeah, been through 'Bama too. Mississippi, yeah. You know what? You eye me worse than those rednecks. They used to look at me in my uniform like I didn't belong in it. (*Struts around in a circle.*) I'd be sharper than sharp. My jump boots spit-shined till my face was lost in them. You could cut your fingers on the creases in my khakis. My brass, my ribbons, they would make their blood boil. They'd turn away, cursing through their teeth. With your eyes pressed against the face-window, you're like a white moon over Stone Mountain. You're everywhere. All I have to go back to are faces just like yours at the door.

Short-timer's Calendar

Like a benediction of blue
feathers, minutes & seconds
moved me beyond who I was
before I knew I could snap,
seeing each hour worked down to salt
under a white grinding stone.
I'd lie awake listening to insects
closing another season,
& recounting tick marks
on the back of a lover's photograph—
where *now* meets *then*. Another day
gone, a few more young faces
dissolving from the formation.
Sometimes I wrestled their ghosts
in my sleep, with the Southern Cross
balanced on a branch weighing a cloud
of sparrows. Back in August
Sarge said, "If you want to stay
in one piece, don't hang around
short-timers. They just trip
over booby traps." It was like playing
tic-tac-toe with God. Each *x*,
a stitch holding breath together,
a map that went nowhere—
like lies told to trees.
I watched them grow into an ink blot,
an omen, a sign the dead could read.

Thanks

Thanks for the tree
between me & a sniper's bullet.
I don't know what made the grass
sway seconds before the Viet Cong
raised his soundless rifle.
Some voice always followed,
telling me which foot
to put down first.
Thanks for deflecting the ricochet
against that anarchy of dusk.
I was back in San Francisco
wrapped up in a woman's wild colors,
causing some dark bird's love call
to be shattered by daylight
when my hands reached up
& pulled a branch away
from my face. Thanks
for the vague white flower
that pointed to the gleaming metal
reflecting how it is to be broken
like mist over the grass,
as we played some deadly
game for blind gods.
What made me spot the monarch
writhing on a single thread
tied to a farmer's gate,
holding the day together
like an unfingered guitar string,
is beyond me. Maybe the hills
grew weary & leaned a little in the heat.
Again, thanks for the dud
hand grenade tossed at my feet
outside Chu Lai. I'm still
falling through its silence.

I don't know why the intrepid
sun touched the bayonet,
but I know that something
stood among those lost trees
& moved only when I moved.

To Have Danced with Death

The black sergeant first class
who stalled us on the ramp
didn't kiss the ground either.

When two hearses sheened up to the plane
& government silver-gray coffins
rolled out on silent chrome coasters,

did he feel better? The empty left leg
of his trousers shivered as another hearse
with shiny hubcaps inched from behind a building . . .

his three rows of ribbons rainbowed
over the forest of faces through
plate glass. Afternoon sunlight

made surgical knives out of chrome
& brass. He half smiled when
the double doors opened for him

like a wordless mouth taking back promises.
The room of blue eyes averted his.
He stood there, searching

his pockets for something:
maybe a woman's name & number
worn thin as a Chinese fortune.

I wanted him to walk ahead,
to disappear through glass,
to be consumed by music

that might move him like Sandman Sims,
but he merely rocked on his good leg
like a bleak & soundless bell.

Report from the Skull's Diorama

Dr. King's photograph
comes at me from *White Nights*
like Hoover's imagination at work,

dissolving into a scenario
at Firebase San Juan Hill:
our chopper glides in closer,
down to the platoon of black GIs
back from night patrol

with five dead. Down
into a gold whirl of leaves
dust-deviling the fire base.
A field of black trees
stakes down the morning sun.

With the chopper blades
knife-fighting the air,
yellow leaflets quiver
back to the ground, clinging to us.
These men have lost their tongues,

but the red-bordered
leaflets tell us
VC didn't kill
Dr. Martin Luther King.
The silence etched into their skin

is also mine. Psychological
warfare colors the napalmed hill
gold-yellow. When our gunship
flies out backwards, rising
above the men left below

to blend in with the charred
landscape, an AK-47
speaks, with the leaflets
clinging to the men & stumps,
waving to me across the years.

Combat Pay for Jody

I counted trip flares
the first night at Cam Ranh Bay,
& the molten whistle of a rocket
made me sing her name into my hands.
I needed to forget the sea
between us, the other men.
Her perfume still crawled
my brain like a fire moth,
& it took closing a dead man's eyes
to bring the war's real smell
into my head. The quick fire
danced with her nude reflection,
& I licked an envelope each month
to send blood money,
kissing her lipstick mouth-prints
clustering the perfumed paper,
as men's voices collected
in the gray weather I inhaled.
Her lies saved me that year.
I rushed to the word
Love at the bottom of a page.
One day, knowing a letter waited,
I took the last chopper back to Chu Lai,
an hour before the fire base was overrun
by NVA. Satchel charges
blew away the commander's bunker,
& his men tried to swim the air.
A week later when I returned
to Phoenix, the city hid her
shadow & I couldn't face myself
in the mirror. I asked her used-to-be
if it was just my imagination,

since I'd heard a man
could be boiled down to his deeds.
He smiled over his wine glass
& said, "It's more, man.
Your money bought my new Chevy."

Sunset Threnody

She's here again. There
leaning against the basement
window where the sun
crouches like a tiger.
Shaking the ice in her glass
to beckon the waitress
for another Tom Collins,
she knows an old wound starts to tingle
close to the heart.

Midwestern prom queen,
Army nurse, now working
the graveyard shift at St. Luke's
emergency ward, sweet thing
for every Vietnam vet.
How many faces are hers?
I've unhealed myself
for her eyes.

All the close calls
are inside my head
bright as a pinball machine,
& I'm a man fighting
with myself. Yes, no,
yes. I'm crouched there
in that same grassy gully
watching medevac choppers
glide along the edge
of the South China Sea,

down to where men run
with a line of green canvas
stretchers as twilight sinks
into the waves. I'm still
there & halfway to her
table where she sits
holding the sun
in her icy glass.

After the Fall

An afternoon storm has hit
the Pearl of the Orient
& stripped nearly everybody.
Bandoliers, miniskirts, tennis shoes,
fatigue jackets, combat boots—
city colors are bruised & polyester
suits limp down side streets.
Even the ragpicker is glad
to let his Australian bush hat
with the red feather float away.

Something deeper than sadness
litters the alleys like the insides
kicked out of pillows.
The old mama-san who always
collected scraps of yellow paper,
cigarette butts, & matchsticks
through field-stripped years
hides under her cardboard box.
Cowboys park new Harleys
along Lam Son Square

& disappear with gold in their mouths.
Dzung leaves the Continental Hotel
in a newspaper dress.
Hoping for a hard rain,
she moves through broken colors
flung to the ground,
mixing up the words to Trinh's
"Mad Girl's Love Song"
& "Stars Fell on Alabama,"
trying to bite off her tongue.

Saigon Bar Girls, 1975

You're among them
    washing off makeup
    & slipping into peasant clothes
    the color of soil.
    Chu nom lotus
rooted in singing blood,
  I know your story
    molded from ashes
    into a balled fist
      hidden in raw silk.
You're on Tu Do Street
  with whores. Unmirrored,
    they sigh & forget
    their lists of Mikes,
        Bills, Joes, & Johns,
  as they shed miniskirts
    thinner than memories
denied, letting them fall
    into a hush
    at their feet—
French perfume
pale as history, reverie
  of cloth like smoke rings
blown at an electric fan.

Ho Xuan Huong,
  you can now speak.
  Those Top 40 hits
have been given to a gale
  moving out to sea,
  no match
for your voice shiny as a knife
against bamboo shoots.
  Bar girls give you

their hard-earned stories
& you pay them
with green shadows
dancing nude around egrets
in paddies where lovers died.
        They stand like Lot's wife
    at plaintive windows
    or return to home villages
        as sleepwalkers, leaving
sloe gin glasses
kissed with lipstick.

Toys in a Field

Using gun mounts
for monkey bars,
Vietnamese children
play skin-the-cat,
pulling themselves through—
suspended in doorways
of multimillion-dollar helicopters
abandoned in white-elephant
graveyards. With arms
spread-eagled they imitate
vultures landing in fields.
Their play is silent
as distant rain,
the volume turned down
on the six o'clock news,
except for the boy
with American eyes
who keeps singing
rat-a-tat-tat, hugging
a broken machine gun.

Boat People

After midnight they load up.
A hundred shadows move about blindly.
Something close to sleep
hides low voices drifting
toward a red horizon. Tonight's
a black string, the moon's pull—
this boat's headed somewhere.
Lucky to have gotten past
searchlights low-crawling the sea,
like a woman shaking water
from her long dark hair.

Twelve times in three days
they've been lucky,
clinging to each other in gray mist.
Now Thai fishermen gaze out across
the sea as it changes color,
hands shading their eyes
the way sailors do,
minds on robbery & rape.
Sunlight burns blood-orange.

Storm warnings crackle on a radio.
The Thai fishermen turn away.
Not enough water for the trip.
The boat people cling to each other,
faces like yellow sea grapes,
wounded by doubt & salt.
Dusk hangs over the water.
Seasick, they daydream Jade Mountain
a whole world away, half-drunk
on what they hunger to become.

Dui Boi, Dust of Life

You drifted from across the sea
under a carmine moon,
framed now in my doorway
by what I tried to forget.
Curly-headed & dark-skinned,
you couldn't escape
eyes taking you apart.
Come here, son, let's see
if they castrated you.

Those nights I held your mother
against me like a half-broken
shield. The wind's refrain
etched my smile into your face—
is that how you found me?
You were born disappearing.
You followed me, blameless
as a blackbird in Hue
singing from gutted jade.

Son, you were born with dust
on your eyelids, but you bloomed up
in a trench where stones were
stacked to hold you down.
With only your mother's name,
you've inherited the inchworm's
foot of earth. *Dui boi.*
I blow the dust off my hands
but it flies back in my face.

Missing in Action

Men start digging in the ground,
propping shadows against trees
outside Hanoi, but there aren't
enough bones for a hash pipe.
After they carve new names
into polished black stone,
we throw dust to the wind
& turn faces to blank walls.

Names we sing in sleep & anger
cling to willows like river mist.
We splice voices on tapes
but we can't make one man
walk the earth again.
Not a single song comes alive
in the ring of broken teeth
on the ground. Sunlight
presses down for an answer.
But nothing can make that C-130
over Hanoi come out of its spin,
spiraling like a flare in green sky.

After the flag's folded,
the living fall
into each other's arms.
They've left spaces
trees can't completely fill.
Pumping breath down tunnels
won't help us bring ghosts
across the sea.

Peasants outside Pakse City
insist the wildflowers
have changed colors.

They're what the wind
& rain have taken back,
what love couldn't recapture.
Now less than a silhouette
grown into the parrot perch,
this one died looking up at the sky.

Losses

After Nam he lost himself,
    not trusting his hands
      with loved ones.

His girlfriend left,
    & now he scouts the edge of town,
      always with one ear

cocked & ready to retreat,
    to blend with hills, poised
      like a slipknot

becoming a noose.
    Unlike punji stakes,
      his traps only snag the heart.

Sometimes he turns in a circle
    until a few faces from Dak To
      track him down.

A dress or scarf in the distance
    can nail him to a dogwood.
      Down below, to his left,

from where the smog rises,
    a small voice reaches his ear
      somehow. No, never mind—

he's halfway back, closer to a ravine,
    going deeper into saw vines,
      in behind White Cove,

following his mind like a dark lover,
    away from car horns & backfire
      where only days are stolen.

Between Days

Expecting to see him anytime
coming up the walkway
through blueweed & bloodwort,
she says, "That closed casket
was weighed down with stones."
The room is as he left it
fourteen years ago, everything
freshly dusted & polished
with lemon oil. The uncashed
death check from Uncle Sam
marks a passage in the Bible
on the dresser, next to the photo
staring out through the window.
"Mistakes. Mistakes. Now,
he's gonna have to give them this
money back when he gets home.
But I wouldn't. I would
let them pay for their mistakes.
They killed his daddy. & Janet,
she & her three children
by three different men, I hope
he's strong enough to tell her
to get lost. Lord, mistakes."
His row of tin soldiers
lines the window sill. The sunset
flashes across them like a blast.
She's buried the Silver Star
& flag under his winter clothes.
The evening's first fireflies
dance in the air like distant tracers.
Her chair faces the walkway
where she sits before the TV
asleep, as the screen dissolves
into days between snow.

Facing It

My black face fades,
hiding inside the black granite.
I said I wouldn't,
dammit: No tears.
I'm stone. I'm flesh.
My clouded reflection eyes me
like a bird of prey, the profile of night
slanted against morning. I turn
this way—the stone lets me go.
I turn that way—I'm inside
the Vietnam Veterans Memorial
again, depending on the light
to make a difference.
I go down the 58,022 names,
half-expecting to find
my own in letters like smoke.
I touch the name Andrew Johnson;
I see the booby trap's white flash.
Names shimmer on a woman's blouse
but when she walks away
the names stay on the wall.
Brushstrokes flash, a red bird's
wings cutting across my stare.
The sky. A plane in the sky.
A white vet's image floats
closer to me, then his pale eyes
look through mine. I'm a window.
He's lost his right arm
inside the stone. In the black mirror
a woman's trying to erase names:
No, she's brushing a boy's hair.

About the Author

Born in the rural community of Bogalusa, Louisiana, Yusef Komun-
yakaa served in Vietnam as a correspondent and editor of *The Southern
Cross* and received a Bronze Star for his service as a journalist. He grad-
uated magna cum laude from the University of Colorado in 1975, com-
pleted his masters degree in 1978 at Colorado State University, and
earned an MFA from The University of California at Irvine in 1980.

The author of nine collections of poetry, Komunyakaa won both the
Pulitzer Prize and the Kingsley Tufts Prize for his book *Neon Vernacular*
(Wesleyan, 1994). He has also been awarded the Thomas Forcade
Award, the William Faulkner Prize, the Levinson Prize from *Poetry*
magazine, the Hanes Poetry Prize, the Ruth Lilly Poetry Prize, and the
Morton Dauwen Zabel Award from the American Academy of Arts
and Letters. In 1999, he was elected a Chancellor of the Academy of
American Poets and was awarded the Shelley Memorial Prize by the
Poetry Society of America.

Komunyakaa has taught at Indiana State University, Washington Uni-
versity, University of California at Berkeley, and the University of New
Orleans, and is currently Professor in the Council of Humanities and
Creative Writing at Princeton University.